BFI FILM CLASSICS

· ·

Edward Buscombe

S E R I E S   E D I T O R

Cinema is a fragile medium. Many of the great classic films of the past now exist, if at all, in damaged or incomplete prints. Concerned about the deterioration in the physical state of our film heritage, the National Film and Television Archive, a Division of the British Film Institute, has compiled a list of 360 key films in the history of the cinema. The long-term goal of the Archive is to build a collection of perfect show-prints of these films, which will then be screened regularly at the Museum of the Moving Image in London in a year-round repertory.

BFI Publishing has now commissioned a series of books to stand alongside these titles. Authors, including film critics and scholars, film-makers, novelists, historians and those distinguished in the arts, have been invited to write on a film of their choice, drawn from the Archive's list. Each volume will present the author's own insights into the chosen film, together with a brief production history and a detailed filmography, notes and bibliography. The numerous illustrations have been specially made from the Archive's own prints.

With new titles published each year, the BFI Film Classics series is rapidly growing into an authoritative and highly readable guide to the great films of world cinema.

Celia Johnson

BFI FILM CLASSICS

BRIEF ENCOUNTER

·····················

Richard Dyer

BRITISH FILM INSTITUTE

bfi

BFI PUBLISHING

First published in 1993 by the
BRITISH FILM INSTITUTE
21 Stephen Street, London W1P 1PL

The British Film Institute exists
to encourage the development of film, television
and video in the United Kingdom,
and to promote knowledge, understanding and
enjoyment of the culture of the moving image.
Its activities include the National Film and
Television Archive; the National Film Theatre;
the Museum of the Moving Image;
the London Film Festival; the production and
distribution of film and video; funding and support for
regional activities; Library and Information Services;
Stills, Posters and Design; Research,
Publishing and Education; and the monthly
Sight and Sound magazine.

British Library Cataloguing in Publication Data

Richard, Dyer
    Brief Encounter – (Film Classics Series)
    I. Title   II. Series
    791.43

    ISBN 0–85170–362–3

Designed by
Andrew Barron & Collis Clements Associates

Typesetting by
Fakenham Photosetting Limited, Norfolk

Printed in Great Britain by
The Trinity Press, Worcester

CONTENTS

. . . .

To Kay Dyer

ACKNOWLEDGMENTS

It will be evident that many people's feelings and thoughts are incorporated into my discussion in these pages. I thank them all and hope that those that recognise themselves do not feel traduced. I should also like to thank Lidia Curti, Ann Kaplan, Tytti Soila and Marina Vitale for inviting me to teach *Brief Encounter* with them, Charlotte Brunsdon, Gill Frith, Simon Frith, Hilary Hinds, Andy Medhurst, Victor Perkins, Jackie Stacey and Ginette Vincendeau for drawing my attention to *Brief Encounter* critiques, mentions, memorabilia and related material, and Jackie and Hilary, and José Arroyo, for their incisive and supportive comments on the first draft.

David Lean (centre) directing Celia Johnson and Trevor Howard

A LOVELY FILM

My mother has two kinds of favourite film, the good and the lovely. The good – pronounced with a drawn-out relish speaking of strong, meaty emotions – are dramas of passion, turbulence and ferocity, Bette Davis, Joan Crawford, Barbara Stanwyck, *Gone With the Wind*, *Gaslight* and *The Flesh is Weak*. Lovely films, on the other hand, present a world of nice people, good manners and comfortable refinement, *Mrs Miniver*, *Random Harvest* and *The Glass Mountain*, anything with Anna Neagle. The two films I most recently saw with her were the good *The Silence of the Lambs* and the lovely *Howard's End* (though to be honest she didn't think much to either of them). *Brief Encounter* is undoubtedly a lovely film, but with such a pull of yearning emotionality that it is also pretty much a good one too.

The first time I remember seeing it was at the National Film Theatre in London in the mid-1960s with my mother and her friend Andy, a woman of strong opinions. I knew of it as one of my mother's lovely films, which at the time I rather despised, too genteel, too English. Yet I was surprised to find that I enjoyed *Brief Encounter*. I recall going not long after with Jeremy, my best friend at school, on a day trip to nearby Croydon, a real towny town with a large store that, like the Kardomah café in the film, had a tea room with a musical trio, and saying to him that, even though it was of course sentimental and frightfully middle-class, it was also, in my view, really quite good, with a superb handling of technique and a wonderful capturing of a certain kind of small-town ambiance.

Even though! I don't think I was denying the pleasure I would later get from it, the good cry I so gladly have; I don't think I felt that at the time. My views were the kind a sixth-former, shedding a petit-bourgeois upbringing for induction into elite culture, was liable to have. I hadn't read anything about this film, as far as I can remember, and I'm not even sure I'd got on to Dilys Powell or *The Film Till Now*, but somehow I'd picked up the prevalent critical discourses about realism and the inventive use of technique, and seen that *Brief Encounter* did well on both counts. Jeremy was more severe and, since he seemed ahead of the critical game, impressed on me the deadly respectability of its reputation.

I don't remember seeing it again until I started teaching. I began using it to open courses on British cinema, as an example of what this is commonly taken to be. With the orthodox daring of the film education of the day (the mid-70s), the point of the courses was to show that there was so much else to British cinema and that this had been marginalised by the likes of *Brief Encounter*. I used the film in this way with a number of groups. Notable was an Adult Education class at Keele University, nearly all of whom were older than me. On the one hand, their feelings of attachment and rejection towards the film were more intense than mine, there was more invested in it for them (or so it seemed then), which made me remember how alive the film could be for people, as it had been for my mother. On the other hand, they also loved doing film studies, loved picking over the film in detail, and so made me see both how rewarding it was to do this with *Brief Encounter* and also how one could perfectly well bring together strong emotional response to a film and itsy-bitsy textual analysis of it.

I also used the film in teaching abroad, in the USA, Italy and Sweden. In Naples they hated it. 'All that suffering, and for what?', they cried. Even those who thought it well done also thought it appalling. They couldn't understand why Laura and Alex didn't just get on and have sex, and why indeed she didn't leave Fred for him. Their revulsion did occasion an immediate bond with a graduate student who intervened to remark feelingly that there were worse things in life than dull husbands; but on the whole they all thought it awful. I do see why: the pressures on Laura now seem unnecessary or unacceptable, in an age where heterosexual sex is less momentous than it was when ineluctably tied to procreation, where divorce is commonplace, where women feeling passionate, and libidinous, is taken for granted. It is salutary to be reminded how embedded in its time the film is. And yet I also feel that many of the emotions it mobilises are not in fact things of the past: betrayal and deception, divided loyalties, the pull between safety and excitement, cosiness and abandon.

Jeremy's stern judgment meant that when I started teaching the film, it was as a specimen, not really to do with me. Yet over the years the experience of teaching it brought the specimen to life. Meanwhile, alongside this, the film took on a new life for me as an item of gay sensibility. I don't know when I first started noticing how many other gay men loved the film, or when so many phrases from the film ('My dear, I've been shopping till I'm dropping', 'There go me Banburys all over the floor') became part of the vocabulary of my gay household, or when my friend Malcolm came up with the notion of he and I doing the whole thing in the 'Travellers' Fare' at Birmingham New Street Station, a plan that came to nothing as we could never agree which of us would be Laura, and I want to be Dolly as well. Someone I met wanted to call his autobiography *There Aren't Any Pantomimes in June*, after the forlorn utterance of Laura's daughter, Margaret. A bar in London, popular with well dressed, worked-out gay men, is called 'Brief Encounter'; I once suggested meeting my friend Hugh there, but he said he couldn't bear it, it was so very 'Brief Encounter', if I knew what he meant, and for some reason I did. For years I wanted to do a remake of it, starring Jane Fonda as Laura and Barbra Streisand as the lover, and ending on a freeze-frame of Jane opening her front door but twisting her body yearningly back towards Barbra. Now there is a gay remake in Richard Kwietniowski's characteristically witty and stylish *Flames of Passion* (1990).

I have presented the presence of *Brief Encounter* in gay discourse in a campy way, but this is itself a characteristically gay way of handling powerfully emotional material. (Needless – no, necessary – to say that not all homosexual men participate in gay culture.) For *Brief Encounter* also makes us cry. The subject matter – forbidden love in ordinary lives – makes an obvious appeal to gay readers, as do fear of discovery and settling for respectability (Laura's home is her closet). As Andy Medhurst puts it, *Brief Encounter* 'explores the pain and grief caused by having one's desires destroyed by the pressures of social convention and it is this set of emotions which has sustained its reputation in gay subcultures.'[1] Medhurst's concern in the article from which this is taken is not just the possibility of appropriating *Brief Encounter* in a gay way – at once campy and for real – but that it is also an instance of gay cultural production (specifically through the input of producer and scenarist Noël Coward). In other words, if *Brief Encounter* feels gay to me and many other gay people that I know, it is because it was made with gay feeling.

It is a truth universally acknowledged that all gay men love their mothers. Yet I sometimes feel that I betray mine with *Brief Encounter*. I recall one Christmas showing it on tape to a group of Australian and Canadian gay men, whose education in the foundations of gay sensibility had revealed a troubling gap. My mother watched it with us and I could see that she was uncomfortable with my doing Laura's lines over Celia Johnson, because it was mocking a lovely film. It was also mocking, or at any rate pastiching, a woman. Yet, like many gay men, I ardently identify with women characters in 'women's films', I prefer the company of women to that of men and I think of myself as pro-feminist. Do I betray this as much as my mother when I camp about with *Brief Encounter*?

The film has in fact divided feminists in my generation. Sue Aspinall, for instance, finds it 'a powerful film' which 'states the contradiction between sexual desire and stable child-rearing arrangements with quiet force',[2] whereas Antonia Lant argues that in *Brief Encounter* 'a woman's dilemma is aired within the terms of realism, subtly suggesting that women are naturally ineffective ... and unable to control ... their own destinies'.[3]

These different readings have in part to do with the nature of *Brief Encounter* itself. It is a film for women made by men. It thus affords opportunities for empowerment (for women to take the film as theirs) and tendencies towards subordination (men determining women's position). It offers an outsiders' view of women's lives, with all the potential which that offers for sympathy and clear-sightedness as well as incomprehension and offence. It has been important for me in both thinking about feminist critiques of the cinema and in negotiating the ambiguity of my own relation to women, both feeling a sense of identity with them yet also acknowledging the stubborn fact that I am not one. Being 'inside' and 'outside' a film simultaneously seems to me a necessary critical stance, but there's also much invested in that for me in the case of *Brief Encounter*.

. . . .

Brief Encounter has figured for me in both my personal and my professional life; and now here I am writing a book about it. In what follows, after a short account of the film, I concentrate on the two most obvious qualities of the film: its concern with women and its Englishness. I try to use as checks on each other my personal relation to the film (emotionally involved and campily detached), what others (friends, students and writers) have said of it, the kinds of thinking and feeling that informed it (its context in this sense) and the textual detail of the film itself. In *Brief Encounter*, as I'll argue below, Laura tells her own story from where she is situated, but incorporates the detailed extensiveness of the world she lives in and corrects her account in the light of what others say. I like to think that my method, as just described, is only proceeding as Laura proceeds.

SEVEN THURSDAYS
. . . .

England, the late 1930s. Laura Jesson, by her own account an 'ordinary' and 'happily married' woman, takes the train every Thursday from her home in rural Ketchworth to the town of Milford. She does some shopping, changes her book at the library run by Boots the Chemist, has lunch in the Kardomah café and goes to the pictures. Before catching the train home, she has a cup of tea in the station buffet, where she enjoys the by-play between the ticket collector, Albert Godby, and the buffet manageress, Myrtle Bagot ('the one with the refined voice').

One evening, waiting on the platform, Laura gets a piece of grit in her eye. A man she doesn't know, a doctor called Alec Harvey, removes it for her and they catch their trains. 'That's how it all began, just through me getting a little piece of grit in my eye. I completely forgot the whole incident. It didn't mean anything to me at all. At least I didn't think it did.'

The next Thursday they bump into each other outside Boots and exchange pleasantries.

Well, I must be getting along to the hospital.

And I must be getting along to the grocer's.

What exciting lives we lead, don't we?

That evening at the station she glances at Alec's train pulling out, wondering vaguely if he is on it.

The Thursday after, she and Alec both happen to lunch at the Kardomah and as it is crowded they share a table. He explains that he comes to Milford every Thursday to cover for Stephen Lynn, the chief physician at the hospital, and she tells him of the pattern of her weekly visits. He decides to take the afternoon off and go to the pictures with her. Afterwards they have a cup of tea at the station before taking their respective trains home; he tells her about his 'special pigeon', preventative medicine, and their eyes meet as he talks. He asks her to join him the next Thursday at the same time.

No I couldn't possibly.

Please – I ask it most humbly.

You'll miss your train.

All right.

Run!

Goodbye.

I'll be there!

When she gets home, she finds that her son Bobbie has had a slight accident with a car. She is mortified, as if it is her fault, although he is soon sitting up in bed enjoying being made a fuss of. After dinner, she tells Fred, her husband, about having lunch and going to the pictures with Alec. 'Good for you!' says Fred and she laughs to think she has taken the whole thing so seriously.

Next week she waits for Alec at the Kardomah, meaning to say they shouldn't meet again, but he doesn't come. She goes to the pictures and has tea alone. Just as his train is about to leave, he comes running in, explains why he couldn't join her, catches his train and asks to see her next Thursday.

Next Thursday, the fifth in succession. They leave the big picture, *Flames of Passion*, halfway through and go boating on the lake in the Botanic Gardens. Alec falls in and has to dry out in the boatman's shed over a cup of tea. He tells her he's fallen in love with her and she admits that it is the same for her. At the station, in the underpass, they kiss for the first time; in the train home, she fantasises about their relationship. At home, feeling guilty for having spent the day with Alec, she tells Fred that she had lunch with a friend, Mary Norton, and then rings Mary to ask her to cover for her.

The following week – week six – they have lunch at the Royal Hotel. On the way out, they meet Mary Norton and her cousin Hermione, who have also been lunching there. Alec has borrowed a car from Stephen Lynn and they drive out into the country. At the station, he tells her he is going back to Stephen's flat (Stephen being away) and asks her to join him. She refuses but, just as her train is about to pull out, she changes her mind and goes to the flat. Almost immediately, however, Stephen unexpectedly comes back, feeling unwell. Laura sneaks out before he can see her, though not before he has heard 'the rather undignified scuffling' of her departure. She runs through the streets, rings Fred to explain that she is late because, she lies, she is comforting the Boots librarian, Miss Lewis, whose mother has been taken ill, and winds up sitting by the town war memorial. Back at the station, she persuades the assistant waitress, Beryl, to stay open long enough for her to have a brandy and write a note. Alec joins her and tries to comfort her.

We know we really love each other. That's true. That's all that really matters.

It isn't all that really matters. Other things matter too, self-respect matters, and decency – I can't go on any longer.

He tells her that he has been offered a job in Johannesburg and they realise that this is the best way for them to bring the relationship to a real end.

The next Thursday, their last together, they again go into the country. Waiting at the station buffet for the last time, they are joined by a friend of Laura's, Dolly Messiter, and are thus unable to savour their last few minutes together. After he has gone, Laura goes out on to the platform, wanting to throw herself under the express train, but is unable to go through with it. Back home, Laura goes over the events of the past seven weeks in her mind, silently telling Fred of the affair.

The film shows us first Dolly joining Laura and Alec, and Laura going home, and then, in a long flashback, the story of the brief encounter.

THAT FEMININE ANGLE
·························

In 1949 Catherine de la Roche wrote in the *Penguin Film Review* complaining of film-makers producing films with 'that feminine angle', which insult the real tastes and concerns of women.[4] Two years before, E. Arnot Robertson had made a similar point. However, while she singled out *Brief Encounter* as 'blessedly adult, truthful and contemporary',[5] de la Roche (elsewhere) found it limited by its 'mask of realism'.[6] In effect, for Robertson the film did give women a voice, for de la Roche it didn't (or only within strict limitations).

There has always been this disagreement over the film, and it is in part inevitable. *Brief Encounter* is a film made almost entirely by men, most of whose story is told by a woman. Behind the camera, men authored the film; on camera, a woman does. One cannot prove one way or the other whether such a case must always only be how men imagine women imagine, but one can analyse the way the film places a woman as story-teller. To what extent does the film, in Marcia Landy's words, reproduce 'the plight of the female seeking a voice, while at the same time silencing her'?[7] To what extent does she tell the story? Is her telling given the authority of truth? What are the circumstances that make it possible for a woman to be something rare in film, the teller of a tale?

What, in short, is the film's feminine angle? I'm going to suggest that the film is very insistent that Laura is the reliable teller of her own story. There is a price to be paid for being granted this authority: Laura speaks as one subjected to male judgment and moreover is not listened to, in the film. Yet certain things – notably Celia Johnson's performance and Laura's reading habits – also provide a space for the articulation of a woman's view at variance with male perceptions.

....

The story of Laura's encounter with Alec is introduced into the film by her voice. Even before we see it unfolded, her voice effectively gives us a blurb or trailer for it (both are appropriate given Laura's cultural life), in the form (equally appropriately) of a confession: 'I'm a happily married woman – or rather, I was, until a few weeks ago. [...] But, oh, Fred, I've been so foolish. I've fallen in love.' Then the telling proper of the story begins with her voice-over signalling the fact in now-here's-the-story fashion: 'It all started on ...' Only at this point do we begin to see the story, the images ushered in by Laura's words.

What's more, the story continues to be told by Laura's voice even while it is being shown on screen – often to the point of redundancy. We don't need to be told that she changed her book at Boots, or that she and Alec stood on a bridge and looked down into the water, or that he pressed her shoulder when he left for the last time, because we can see for ourselves that these things were so. One effect of such redundant voice-over narration, however, is to insist that this long flashback is not just a device for telling one story in the context of another, but is specifically Laura's telling of it.

This is reinforced by the use of music, Rachmaninov's second piano concerto. This music, by turns turbulent, yearning and melancholy, also, by taking the form of the romantic piano concerto, expresses the idea of the individual (the soloist) seized by overwhelming emotions. The fact that the well-known pianist Eileen Joyce is announced in the credits as the soloist, that she provided the playing (including part of the same concerto) for an even greater success of the same year, *The Seventh Veil*, and that both the latter and *Love Story* (a year earlier) centre on the emotional turmoil of a woman pianist, all give a particular female inflection to the music. The fact that all play music composed by men reproduces the central problem of the 'feminine angle'.

In *Brief Encounter*, the Rachmaninov is entirely associated with Laura. Apart from being played over the credits, it is first heard during her and Dolly's train journey home; it seeps in as the camera moves very slowly into an extreme close-up of her and we hear her voice-over for the first time. When Dolly interrupts her thoughts, the music stops, only to be reintroduced when the camera again moves in on her, with the light darkening around her, and she carries on with her internal monologue. Similarly, when Laura phones Fred, after the debacle in Stephen Lynn's flat, the music stops the moment she gets through to Fred and starts again the moment she hangs up. In both cases, the music is associated with her and positively dissociated from anyone else. And of course, when she looks for some music on the radio, she chooses Rachmaninov over dance music or French speech.

Rachmaninov and voice-over function as signals that what we are seeing we are seeing through Laura. It is not possible to distinguish in their use her thoughts and feelings during the encounter from what she now thinks and feels. For instance, after she says goodbye to Alec at the end of their first day together, she walks pensively on the platform and we hear her voice, and Rachmaninov, telling of what she was thinking, about his going home, his *not* telling his wife about meeting 'such a nice woman at the Kardomah' and 'the first awful feeling of danger' sweeping over her. This is recollection: the voice uses the past tense, the music has been established as the sound of reverie and is, besides, on the radio at home; yet it is also immediately and concretely before us, and more generally in films voice-over and background music are well established devices of interiority and emotional expressivity. In short, what we get, throughout the film, insists that it is Laura's view of her brief liaison with Alec, how it was for her then, how it is for her now.

Yet there are points in the film when what we get is either what she cannot know or what we can know she has got wrong. The most important case of the former is the conversation between Alec and Stephen, after Laura has fled the flat on hearing the latter's return; she cannot possibly know what transpired, and her ignorance is reinforced by her speculating on it to Alec ('I suppose he laughed, didn't he? I suppose you spoke of me together as men of the world') and his denial ('We didn't speak of you'). But we the audience have seen and heard their conversation. Equally, there is the case of where we see, in her telling of it, what we have previously seen independently of her narration: the lovers' final moments together, Dolly's interruption and Laura's suicide attempt (the latter only made clear in the repeat). In at least two small particulars the second (flashback) version does not exactly repeat the first. When the loudspeaker announces Alec's train, we hear the whole of it in the second version with all three of them sitting silent throughout it, whereas they only stop speaking at, and we only hear, the tail end of it in the first. Secondly, in the flashback version, when Alec leaves, Dolly changes her seat, interrupting Laura's gaze at the door after him; there is no sign that she does this in the first version.

What are we to make of such discrepancies, and Laura's telling what she cannot know? Is she an unreliable narrator? If one thinks she is, a whole range of interpretive possibilities opens up and it is these I want to explore next. However, I don't believe she is an unreliable narrator and it is the nature of her narrative reliability that I shall explore after that.

It had never occurred to me to question Laura's trustworthiness as a narrator until the idea was raised by the Adult Education group at

Keele. One of them raised the question of Alec – was he really like she thought he was? Did he, indeed, really exist at all? I was so startled at the suggestion that I began a 'Well I really don't feel one can really argue that . . .' line, only to find that at least half the group agreed with their fellow student, and some were even rather surprised that anyone could think otherwise.

Questions as to Laura's reliability take one in two directions, towards the truth of the story she tells and towards her state of mind. The first can be posed with varying degrees of scepticism. The story may be entirely a figment of her imagination; or she may know Alec slightly (for instance having indeed had him remove a piece of grit from her eye and seen him about the place and said hello) but has built this up into something much more; or it may all have happened, except that she has fallen in love with him whereas he just wants to get her back to Stephen Lynn's flat for sex. According to Celia Johnson's biography, Trevor Howard could not understand why, when Alec and Laura are alone in Stephen Lynn's flat, they didn't 'simply . . . get on with their affair';[8] perhaps some audiences pick up on this.

Various details lend credence to these interpretations, most notably the introduction of Alec. Laura just glances at him when he comes in and the camera does not dwell on him. When she gets the grit in her eye, and after the glass of water has failed to remove it, she is in medium close-up, putting her finger to her eye, and then we hear his voice ('Can I help you?') before he enters the frame; the image is brightly lit on the right but darkened on the left, and Alec emerges into the image from the left; there is, then, something insubstantial about this character, whom we hear before we see and who appears in the darkness. Thereafter we are given no access to him independently of Laura, so that he may appear to have no existence apart from her imagination.

At times too Laura may be thought to give the game away about her reliability as a narrator. After the grit removal and Alec's departure, the music comes in (the sign of Laura's emotions) and her voice says, 'I completely forgot the whole incident – it didn't mean anything to me at all – at least I didn't think it did', as if perhaps to say that it was a passing incident which she has built up into something since. Similarly, when Alec puts his arm under hers at the station, her voice says, 'I didn't notice it then, but I remember it now', as if perhaps to let on that she knows she is 'romancing', telling agreeable fictions.

As it happens, I think all of this is explicable without casting doubt on Laura's reliability (she correctly remembers only gradually becoming aware of him; she tells us nothing of this home and work life, beyond his speaking of them, because she knows nothing of them; very subtly, she registers the knowing and not knowing that accompany the awakening of her illicit love). I also find this a useful perspective on Laura's subjectivity, which I'll discuss in a moment. There is, however, a second set of considerations about her reliability, which focus on her state of mind.

One version of this simply stresses that her recollections are told at a time of distress, guilt, longing, of high emotion which must distort her memory. Another way of putting this is to say that Laura is hysterical. In the everyday sense of the word (at the end of her emotional tether) this is only another way of describing her state of high emotion; Laura speaks of being 'hysterical inside' when she gets home from an afternoon with Alec to find that her son has had an

'Can I help you?' Alec removes the grit from Laura's eye

accident, but the very fact that she uses the word indicates how much in common usage it was. However, the word also has a more specifically Freudian meaning, the relevance of which to Laura was argued forcefully to me by a graduate student and is touched on in Antonia Lant's discussion of the film. Hysteria here implies a deep-seated personality disorder, not just a feeling occasioned by immediately distressing circumstances. Laura's desire to commit suicide, her need to rake over the past, her real silence about the past, her anxiety about people looking at her, such factors can be checked off against Freud's writings on hysteria to make her appear a case study. She might be thought to provide ammunition for the diagnosis, when she acknowledges that she is given to 'fainting spells' (like almost anything, part of the symptomology of hysteria) and must be 'that type of woman'.

The fainting spells discussion occurs when Laura is telling Fred what happened at the station. But of course nothing of the sort happened; she tried to commit suicide and when she failed, she was shaken and distressed. Who would not be? It is the reasonableness of her response that is at issue. My problem with the reading of Laura as hysterical is not that of psychoanalysing fictional characters, nor that Freudian ideas of hysteria were not sufficiently in circulation to construct this character as a hysteric (they probably were), nor even the intrinsic validity of psychoanalytic ideas, and *a fortiori* that of the hysterical woman, but that this reading pathologises Laura and, by implication, E. Arnot Robertson, my mother, and the countless women who have found a certain truth in the film. Such pathologising is moreover at odds with the film's insistent construction of Laura as ordinary, not someone with a condition. Laura is *unhappy*; she has just said goodbye forever to a man she loves, has no one to turn to and is racked with guilt about the husband and children she also loves. Unhappiness is an entirely healthy, indeed rational response to her situation.

But what then of the discrepancies in her telling of the tale? These are only a problem if one's notion of reliable narration – and of memory itself – is one of absolute objectivity and transparency, a notion itself based on a concept of knowledge as separate, out there, divorced from human perception, a scientific concept of knowledge that science itself has long questioned. The story of Laura and Alec is seen and told only from Laura's point of view, but that does not mean that it is in some negative sense only what she sees. It is situated knowledge, knowledge that recognises that all knowledge has to be from a particular point of view, that the knower of knowledge is always 'in' that which she or he knows, that to be explicit about where one is in relation to what one knows and tells is as near to being objective as a human can be. In this paradigm of knowledge, as in so many things, I take Laura as my model.

In this perspective, the problems touched on above look different. The account in Laura's flashback of the exchange between Alec and Stephen, an exchange she cannot have seen, must of course be how she imagines it, but significantly she imagines it now in memory differently from how she told Alec she imagined it immediately after ('I suppose you spoke of me together as men of the world'); it is as if she has corrected her idea of it in the light of the evidence available to her (Alec's assurance that 'we spoke of some nameless creature who has no reality at all'). In general, she does not tell us what she does not know. For instance, she does not in memory even try to imagine Madeleine, Alec's wife, whom in conversation with him she admits she'd imagined wrong ('I should've thought she would've been fair'). The very uncertainty that some feel about Alec, his motives, his investment in the relationship, is itself a product of her reliability, the fact that she only says what she knows, which is what he has said and done with her – she inadvertently leaves the gap open for us to have doubts about him (not that I personally do).

On the other hand, the distortions in the repeat of the first scene of the film clearly register Laura's emotions in the sequence: the tension caused by Dolly's presence, so that they all sit in awkward silence listening to the whole of the loudspeaker announcement; the violence of Dolly, seeming literally to come between Laura and her yearning gaze at the door Alec has left through. Given her state of feeling, what is remarkable is that this is all she gets wrong, that everything else is so accurately recalled.

Laura's authority as narrator, and the way the film recognises that all reality is perceived – and really is perceived – through emotion, are not confined to her recollections. They are even true of the opening sequence. The first shot of Laura and Alec together, with the sound of

Albert talking about a guilty passenger, colours the pair with what we
come to know is Laura's feeling about the relationship. The second shot
of them follows an immediate cut from Myrtle saying to Albert, 'Time
and tide wait for no man, Mr Godby.' This shot has them down-screen
left and Dolly entering and greeting Laura ('What a lovely surprise!').
In the repeat of the sequence, we will learn that Dolly cuts in
immediately after Alec has said, 'We've still got a few minutes' (their
last ever together); and, as discussed below, throughout the film the
sense of time, of its pressures, how little there is of it, is reiterated. In
short, Dolly's friendly greeting is caught in a web of associations that
make it indeed, as Laura says at the end, 'cruel'. In these ways even this
section of the film, not narrated by Laura, is still structured by her
feelings about the situation.

A little later, when Alec leaves, there is a close-up of him gently
squeezing her shoulder before going. This is the most obtrusive piece of
camerawork so far in the film, using a close-up to convey a sense of the
momentousness (for Laura) of his departure. It is not a point-of-view
shot, which would explicitly place the gesture within Laura's

Dolly greets Laura: 'What a lovely surprise!'

perception; it is the film as impersonal narration slipping into identification with Laura's personal position. Within and without Laura's narration, the film always presents us with situated knowledge of this story, which it also signals as true knowledge, not distortion or hysterics.

. . . .

Brief Encounter puts a woman at the centre of the story, puts her in charge of telling the story, validates her account and perception of it. Yet there is a price to pay for this position of narrative authority. This has to do with the tone of her narration, its address and implied audience.

It was a student in Naples who first pointed out to me that the whole of the flashback is seen through guilt and remorse. Though there is nothing Catholic about the film, its tone is undoubtedly confessional. Here is no mere nostalgic recall, leave alone recollection in tranquillity: it immediately follows a failed suicide attempt and bursting into tears after dinner; it is triggered by, most distressingly, Fred's crossword

Close-up: Alec squeezes Laura's shoulder

linking romance to delirium, but also by the myriad things that do not allow Laura to forget what she no longer has (Dolly chattering on about the allure of doctors and specifically her use of the word 'passion', which cues Laura's first interior monologue in the film; Fred joking about going to the cinema together, thereby reminding her of what she used to do with Alec; the sound of an express train, evoking the very *mise en scène* of the affair). Laura's voice-over never allows the story, its humour, its sunshine, to exist free of her unhappiness and guilt: 'I had no premonitions although I suppose I should have had' (about laughing with Alec at the Kardomah), 'That should have given me a pang of conscience, I know, but it didn't' (about little boys like Bobbie sailing boats in the park), 'I felt so utterly humiliated and defeated and so dreadfully, dreadfully ashamed.' Even when she tells that she was happy, she brings us back to the fact that she isn't now: 'I felt gay and happy and sort of released – that's what's so shameful about it all'; 'I should have been utterly wretched and ashamed – I know I should, but I wasn't.'

This sense of guilt, shame and unhappiness is all-pervasive, even outside of Laura's narration. As suggested above, the first shot of Alec and Laura together associates them with ideas of guilt. On their first visit to the cinema, she talks brightly of feeling guilty about the extravagance of sitting upstairs, but her face soon clouds with an impending sense of a real reason to be guilty. She describes their leaving *Flames of Passion* before the end 'rather furtively, as though we were committing a crime' (perhaps because they were off to fan their real flames of passion), here not only conflating present and past feeling (did they feel guilty at the time, is that her judgment now, or both?) but also infusing the sombre language of guilty recall with the kind of amusing, slightly arch tone she uses with Alec. Inconsequential bystanders – a clergyman ('I felt myself blushing'), a policeman ('I felt like a criminal') – are figures of guilt that Laura felt then but is also using now in her telling of the story to cast it within the frame of guilt.

These bystanders are, however, not really inconsequential figures. They are precisely the people to whom one confesses in Western society. For the tone of guilt derives not only from the particular use of language but also from the assumed addressee. This is Fred, but it is also patriarchal authority. In an immediate sense, Laura needs to confess to Fred because she loves him and knows that he would be upset if he knew about her and Alec. Yet Fred also represents society and her place in it as 'a happily married woman', a wife and mother. Throughout the film there are others who represent society, its values, what is right and proper, and always they penetrate Laura with remorse.

They are all men. The possible exceptions are Mary Norton and her cousin Hermione, who see Alec and Laura having lunch at the Royal and give probably pointed looks and a suggestive remark ('I do so envy you your champagne'). Laura experiences this as 'awful', saying to Alec, 'they had been watching us all through lunch.' Yet Mary does not function as an authority figure, a mouthpiece of the social order. On the contrary, we have already seen her happily conniving with Laura in deceiving Fred (albeit without reference to adultery); as she does so, on the other end of the telephone, she plucks a hair (or blackhead?) from between her eyebrows with a pair of tweezers, a rather unpleasant gesture and presumably how Laura imagines her, suggesting at a minimum that deceiving husbands is par for the course

Male figures of authority: a clergyman, a policeman

and need not distract one from the business of beautification. What is 'awful' for Laura is to be associated with such a woman, her easy deceitfulness, her oh-so-amused commentary on Laura and Alec.

The men are all in positions of authority, either by virtue of their general social position (clergyman, doctor, policeman) or their gender position in relation to Laura. None actually expresses disapproval; rather, she internalises their views, she feels looked at, judged, found wanting. The clergyman looks at her mildly before returning to his book, but she nonetheless blushes, internalising what he would, properly, think if he knew; the doctor sits by her talking about Bobbie's condition after the accident as her voice tells us she felt 'so dreadful', as if being punished; the policeman asks kindly after her ('You don't want to go and catch cold, you know') but she still feels 'like a criminal'. This reaches its peak in the scene with the policeman (which takes place after her flight from Stephen Lynn's flat). Not only is he present, not only does she have a cigarette and thus transgress, as her voice says, the code of femininity ('I know how you [Fred] disapprove of women smoking in the street – I do too, really'), but she sits at the war

memorial. A high-angle shot has it towering over her, a symbol of male sacrifice in securing the society to which she belongs, and a symbol also, it must be said, of very obvious phallic proportions pointing in her direction (in a quick dissolve, directly at her head). This is, apart from the suicide attempt, perhaps the moment of greatest despair in the film, when she feels the full weight of patriarchal disapproval.

When Alec and Laura kiss in the underpass, they part because a couple come down into it, and immediately Fred's voice interrupts her memory, asking if the music might be turned down a bit. It is the only time he disturbs her reverie and it is at a point of maximum illicitness within it. It is a husbandly call to order. Fred, who is consistently easygoing and pleasant in the film and whom Laura repeatedly says, without reservation, she loves, is nonetheless also another male authority figure. He has knowledge of her and his male rights are not in doubt.

At the end of the film, he knows that something has been up with Laura; he refers to her having had a 'dream' ('It wasn't a very happy one, was it?'). This could refer to her days with Alec, a sort of lived

Laura feels the full weight of patriarchal disapproval

fantasy that brought unhappiness; perhaps he even guesses or knows about the affair. If so, this gives him a total knowledge of her, which however kindly meant and comforting at this point, also suggests she can have no inner or private life to which he does not have access. If all he means, however, is that she has been having miserable thoughts, that she was in this sense 'far away', it is kind of him to be concerned but also just a little excessive to experience a wife having her own thoughts as a withdrawal from him (from being always absorbed in him).

The oppressive undertow to Fred's nonetheless genuine niceness and decency is suggested by the last shot of the film (last, that is, apart from 'The End' over a shot of the railway). It suggests her place as wife in relation to him, and the admixture of security and denial of self in this. He kneels beside her in her armchair, asks if he can help ('You always help,' she says), thanks her for coming back to him. His position, bringing himself down to her level in a kind of supplicating welcome, presents him as gentle and comforting. Yet when she bursts into tears (letting out the emotion of the monologue or moved by Fred's humble gratitude at having her back?) and weeps into his

'Laura's face obliterated by his as the screen fades to black'

shoulder, the camera moves a little closer and it is Fred who fills the image, Laura's face obliterated by his as the screen fades to black. This is comfort but it is also defeat.

It is not only Fred who represents male authority in Laura's life, it is Alec too. When she returns to the station from the war memorial and Alec joins her, she turns away from him so that he can't look at her, as if his is yet another gaze of male authority. He is a doctor, and her immediate thought is of him discussing her with Stephen, 'the chief physician', several rungs up the male hierarchy. It is from these 'men of the world' that she shields herself. Even before this the film inadvertently displays how much Alec speaks for her, presumes to know her. In the Kardomah he is dismissive of her suggestion that she might have 'a tremendous, burning professional talent' for music; his very sure view that she is 'too sane and uncomplicated' miffs her a little ('It does sound a little dull') but she doesn't challenge it (even though we know of her affinity for Rachmaninov). In the buffet, she declines a 'cake or pastry', but he buys her a Bath bun regardless, saying she 'must eat one of these'. When she is reminiscing in the train home, after the scene in the boathouse, she says, 'I had said I loved him.' In fact she has never said it in so many words; rather he gets it out of her, gets her to assent to his view:

> Tell me honestly, please tell me honestly if what I believe is true.
> What do you believe?
> That's it the same with you, that you've fallen in love too.
> Sounds so silly.
> Why?
> I know you so little.
> It is true, though, isn't it?
> Yes, it's true.

In their scenes together he speaks much more than her. When they meet after she has fled Stephen's flat, she expresses her feelings directly:

> Other things [than love] matter too, self-respect matters, and decency – I can't go on any longer.

whereas he speaks at greater length and on behalf of both of them:

> I know what you feel about this evening, I mean about the
> sordidness of it. I know about the strain of our different lives;
> our lives apart from each other. The feeling of guilt, of doing
> wrong, is too strong, isn't it? Too great a price to pay for the
> happiness we have together. I know all this because it's the
> same for me too.

None of this is remarkable; neither Laura nor the film is drawing
attention to the way he commandeers their interchanges and presumes
to know what she thinks and feels; they take it for granted. Indeed, we
might even say it is part of the film's realism that it grasps heterosocial
intercourse with such a sure touch. Alec, for all the charm he has for her
(and had for my mother, but not for me), occupies his place in male
discourse as securely, unreflectingly and unassertively as Fred and all
the other men in the film.

It is to Fred, as husband the most socially privileged of these men
in relation to her, that Laura pours her heart out in shame. The price of
the film's giving her narrative authority is the insistent reminder that
the terms in which she speaks are laid down by men – not by individual
men, but by masculinist discourse itself, carried in the looks, bearing
and clothes of men, in what Laura has so well learnt of male values.

Yet of course she does not pour it all out. She is silent. The price
of her speech is not only the way it cedes authority to men, but also not
being heard. If Fred's manner and words at the close of the film indicate
that he knows what has happened, it is because men just do know, not
because she has told him. Women may speak as long as men don't have
to listen – even when it is only to a refusal of a cake or pastry.

. . . .

But *we* listen. Laura does not speak to us, yet her voice is for us alone.
C.A. Lejeune wrote in 1948 of *Brief Encounter* having 'a peculiar sort of
intimate appeal to the spectator, whispering directly and persuasively to
the individual rather than speaking to an audience as a crowd'.[9] It is
certainly possible to feel that we are that 'wise, kind friend' that Laura
wishes Dolly were. It is partly just because Laura's confession is not

spoken to anyone in the film that we can feel such a special bond with her. The film lets her speak in terms which do not disturb male discourse – she accepts its terms, she is not heard – but by letting her speak to us it also lets other terms and listeners come into play. These include, especially, Celia Johnson and the kind of reading and readers emblematised in the film by the work of Kate O'Brien.

Celia Johnson is probably what most people remember of the film, along with trains and Rachmaninov. She was universally praised (in print) and nominated for an Oscar. Subsequently she has also been the major stumbling block for many, above all for that accent (and the ease with which she uses such dated vernacular). It's one thing for the Queen to speak with all those sharps and diphthongs and that occasional dry archness, quite another for the protagonist of a drama praised for its truth and universality. Mrs Dale, whose fictional diary on BBC radio maintained the tone with such success through the 1950s, had had to go in 1969. Through the 60s and 70s such speech became a cornerstone of satire and camp; I have known audiences giggle their way through the film on account of it and I have not been above adopting it myself ('He's a naice creature', 'Would some music throw you orff your stride?' 'Like a romantic fool!'). I have a sense that it is no longer the problem it was, perhaps because in the 80s cut-glass accents ceased to be unfashionable, perhaps because it is now simply of its period, far enough away from us no longer to need deriding as dated.

What was praised at the time – and this can still hold, even if one finds her ridiculous or unappealing – was Celia Johnson's naturalness. As a more recent trope of advertising would have it, Celia Johnson *is* Laura Jesson. I have often wished that I knew – or was – Celia Johnson, but of course what I meant was that I'd like to have known or been Laura Jesson. Nonetheless, it is rather disconcerting to feel from her biography by her daughter, Kate Fleming, that to be with Celia would have been like being with Laura. This is not just an effect of the writing, though the book opens with an echo of Laura starting to tell her story in *Brief Encounter*: 'The beginning was very ordinary' (compare Laura's 'It all started on an ordinary day, in the most ordinary place in the world'). It is rather in the copious quotations from Johnson's letters to her husband that the voice of Laura Jesson is also heard, not just in the vocabulary but in the rhythm: 'They are all such nice chaps, very polite and gallant and making small jokes in a human way. I like the English and their ways', 'We gave ourselves a fearfully expensive tea at the Berkeley', 'The unit is mostly mad', '[She] is a dear and very funny and nice'.[10] Such similarities are superficial indicators of what Celia Johnson was really like, but they do make clear the very high degree of continuity between her manner off-screen and in *Brief Encounter*. Celia's letters and Laura's narration both deploy the same class dialect, and with equal assurance.

The effect (of Celia being Laura) is reinforced by Johnson's great ease before the camera, seldom requiring retakes, unfazed by filmic procedures. C.A. Lejeune quotes a cameraman saying 'You can do anything with her ... Stick lamps under her nose, she's got such technique, nothing bothers her'.[11] He recognises it as technique, but it comes across as just being herself. It was a quality perceived in her stage work. Fleming summarises what were held to be her characteristics: 'freshness ... a lack of sentimentality, an absence of technical trickiness, a feeling for comedy, intelligence, sensitivity'.[12] The same terms run through the reviews of her films, and especially *Brief Encounter*.

I have emphasised this perception of her, because it suggests the degree to which her voice and presence (Celia Johnson's, Laura Jesson's) in the film could invite the audience in, not treating her as symptom or spectacle but rather as a place from which to view this kind of life. Then the inflections she gives to the script, especially the way common sense and yearning, amusement and despair, eddy across her face, voice and body, come to suggest an inwardness with this situation, a sort of running commentary on it, that is different from her formal presentation of guilt to male authority.

This can be seen if one compares the published script with Johnson's actual speaking of it in the film. The pauses and stresses, the changes in words, the accompanying face and body language, do not so much alter the meaning of what is said as provide a different perspective on it. When, after their first afternoon together, Laura is walking on the platform musing on Alec's return home, she begins to speculate about his wife. Johnson reverses the first three words of the sentence as given in the script, from 'Madeleine, his wife' to 'his wife, Madeleine', and puts a pause before and after the woman's name. The

reversal and the pauses mean that she doesn't run unthinkingly over her but is literally given pause at mentioning her; the pause also draws attention to the name itself, French, thus slightly exotic though not unfamiliar, perhaps hinting at a glamour Laura feels she lacks. She goes on, in the same slightly flat tone, that Madeleine 'would probably be in the hall to meet him', but then after another pause her voice quickens a little as she says 'or perhaps upstairs in her room, not feeling very well' (abandoning the slight pause indicated by the script after 'room'), before slowing again as she uses the words Alec has used of Madeleine, 'small, dark and rather delicate'. It is as if she momentarily warms to imagining Madeleine, not treating her as an unknown quantity but as another woman with whom she can empathise, before falling back on her (Madeleine's) husband's description of her. The perspective, including both jealousy and empathy, is barely sketched, but it far exceeds anything evident in the script; these are things the male confessor figure is not concerned with, but with which a woman might be.

It is not merely a question of voice. In the exchange where, as I've put it, Alec gets out of her the fact that she loves him, he sits on a box, she on the floor; there are various set-ups, but notably one in which the camera looks down on her from over his shoulder, highlighting what is evident throughout, the play of her eyes. He looks steadily at her, but she both looks back into his eyes and yet keeps looking down momentarily away from him. She is held by his gaze, charmed, transfixed or pressurised according to view, but also not wanting to be held, suggesting a gamut of anxieties, misgivings and unwelcome insights.

There is also at least one – telling – moment when I do feel that Johnson strikes a false note. When Alec is going on about his 'special pigeon', her face takes on a dopey expression. At first this expresses Laura's ignorance of medicine but then, imperceptibly, it becomes her enchantment with him as he warms to his subject. Perhaps her dopeyness is meant straight and it feels unconvincing just because it is bad acting, but the unconvincingness is itself suggestive. Laura so obviously *is* intelligent, even if she doesn't know medical terminology; Alec is so obviously delighted to perform to this subservient female audience – isn't it intolerable that Laura should so abase herself? It's not that she might not put on such an expression, but that it is precisely 'put on'. The unconvincingness speaks of the lengths women have to go to please men.

Many of the inflections that I am suggesting can be read into Celia Johnson's seemingly effortless performance also derive from a most significant thing we know about Laura's cultural life: she reads. She always has a book on the go in the station or train; changing her library book is, as she tells Alec, part of her regular Milford pattern. This reading habit suggests the way in which she inhabits, if only in the privacy of reading, a particular set of ways of thinking and feeling, a particular discourse; many who saw the film could read Laura's situation through this discourse, make it (and especially Johnson's performance) speak what Laura's confession cannot.

Laura gets her books from Boots, not the public library, and she is so identified with it that Miss Lewis, the librarian, not only treats her as a favoured customer but is well enough established in her life to be used to Fred as an excuse for being home late. This suggests a penchant for a particular kind of middlebrow fiction aimed at middle-class women.

Held by his gaze, yet not wanting to be held . . .

The cost of borrowing books at Boots placed it between highbrow and lower-class patterns of consumption, and three-quarters of its customers were women.[13] Laura's reading places her within a circuit of readers and writers who, as Nicola Beauman puts it, 'were linked by their mutual "pre-assumptions"; they spoke the same language, were interested in the same kind of things, led the same kind of lives.'[14]

The main thing we know more specifically of Laura's taste is her delight that Miss Lewis has saved the new Kate O'Brien for her. O'Brien's novels are set either in her native Ireland or in continental Europe, and often in the past. We might put this together with Fred saying that Laura is 'a poetry addict' and her recognition of Keats (and hence a certain notion of the poetic), as well as her selection of Rachmaninov and her fantasies of Paris and palm trees, to suggest an essentially romantic discourse. Certainly this is a component of Laura's cultural framework and an important one – we have to believe in the intensity of her yearning for the lure and danger of the affair to work; such romanticism also gives resonances to, for instance, the symbolism of the express, which Laura points out is 'the boat train', carrier of people to foreign parts, before which she is tempted to sacrifice herself, or to her hesitation around the name 'Madeleine', uneasily suggestive of a romantic sophistication Alec already has to hand.

O'Brien's novels are not really romances, however. Much more, like *Brief Encounter* itself, they are about the conflict between romance and everyday life (most notably in *Mary Lavalle* of 1936, which ends with the heroine in a train, travelling away from her great passion towards her dull fiancé). As Beauman observes, one of the key pre-assumptions that Laura's kind of reading makes is that 'marriage and passion are irreconcilable': you can't have the thrill of romance and the comfort of ordinary life.[15] The novels, and *Brief Encounter*, present this in definite class terms: such irreconcilability is a middle-class dilemma, servants and the working class have greater emotional freedom. This is an image deeply rooted in English novels, even beyond Boots, in works as otherwise disparate as Elizabeth Gaskell's *Cranford*, D.H. Lawrence's *Lady Chatterley's Lover* and E.M. Forster's *Maurice*. Likewise, the staff at Milford Junction – Albert and Myrtle, Beryl and Stanley – are presented as far more free and easy, as implicitly and cheerfully immoral, in a way that Laura and Alec could never be. The class specificity of the feminine angle I am trying to delineate could not be clearer than here, and *Brief Encounter*'s class character is something I shall return to in the next section.

Brief Encounter, like these novels, circulates around the irreconcilability of marriage and passion and all that it implies: security and danger, dreariness and excitement, comfort and ecstasy, predictability and uncertainty. No side of the opposition is ever the unalloyed good – comfort and security entail dreariness, excitement and ecstasy entail danger. The opposition is lived in every detail of life. In *A Note in Music* (Rosamund Lehmann, 1930), Grace is struck by 'the reckless endearing folly' of handsome young Hugh, rushing out into the rain without heed for raincoat or umbrella, and dull old husband Tom returning home 'fully equipped with umbrella and burberry'.[16] Nor does the opposition reside only in the choice between husbands and lovers, but in everything. When Fred and Laura discuss Bobbie's future, Laura is equally unhappy at the adventurous prospect of his going to sea and the dull one of his going into an office and her seeing him off 'on the eight-fifty every morning'. Not only are safety and excitement irreconcilable, neither is satisfactory.

It is not just in this thematic structure but in its tone, characterisation and attitude that *Brief Encounter* speaks the same language as the novels Laura would read. E.M. Delafield's *The Way Things Are* (1927) seems almost like a dry run for *Brief Encounter*, and not only because its main character is called Laura (as is quite common in these novels) and her husband Alfred. Its tone mixes yearning and despair with, as one might expect from the author of *The Diary of a Provincial Lady*, a sharp, dry wit; similarly the Laura of *Brief Encounter*, in the midst of racking confession, is still able to be amusing about Mrs Leftwich's hat, buying Fred's present, her own 'silly dreams' (of Venice and palm trees) and Albert and Myrtle. As in *Brief Encounter*, the men in *The Way Things Are* are no better than OK; like Fred, Alfred is solid and amenable (if a little more ill-tempered); like Alec, Duke, the lover, never quite comes into focus, is more an idea, a longing on the edge of the frame, than a palpable character. And the lovers' final scene together is in a tearoom (albeit in a department store, not a station).

In *Forever England*, Alison Light suggests that the ironic stance towards romance of writers like Delafield, Agatha Christie and Daphne du Maurier is one of the ways women of their generation rejected the image of a female role confined to helpless emotionality:

> Ironic dismissal, worldly wisdom, brisk competence and heroic disavowal could all be part of the reaction to the legacy of representations which had seen ladies as the softer and the frailer sex, the medium of the emotions and of 'higher things'.

However, as Light also suggests, 'the intended rejection of romance by superior women did not mean the disappearance of these out-of-bounds feelings. They could and would return under cover . . .'[17] Laura is ironic, worldly ('sensible') and brisk, and it is instructive to recognise these qualities not only in relation to modernity, as Light suggests, but also in relation to the qualities required of civilians, and especially women, by the wartime appeal to national identity, as discussed by Antonia Lant. Yet none of this can banish the aching desire for intensity, for emotional and physical ecstasy, unlooked for though it is for Laura and, for instance, for Agatha in Margaret Kennedy's *The Ladies of Lyndon* (1923) or Harriet in Elizabeth Taylor's *A Game of Hide and Seek* (1951) (a post-war novel that seems in its use of dirty trains and railway stations at dusk deliberately to echo *Brief Encounter*'s *mise en scène*).

I don't know if *Brief Encounter* consciously drew on the tones and themes of this kind of women's fiction. What I want to argue, rather, is that by having a protagonist who is part of the readership of such novels (like some of the audience), by having her played by someone who seems so at home within this class-specific gender discourse, by having her speak her thoughts and feelings silently but intimately (like a book to a reader), the film could be read through – seems to be expressive of – the nuances and intensities provided by this cultural framework within which women spoke to women. The film itself, by its insistence on Laura narrating her own story, by its casting of Celia Johnson and its realist detailing of Laura's literary taste, provided (some of) the audience with a way of understanding the situation that runs counter to Laura's submission to masculinist cultural frameworks and the destiny of not being listened to. The contradiction may even help us to see this masculinist framework, in Alec's pressurising, in Fred's complacent assurance, in the way clergymen, policemen and doctors are bearers of the discourse of male values, whether they will or no, and so on.

....

Three times Fred says to Laura, 'Have it your own way': after their discussion about whether to take the children to the circus or the pantomime, when she refuses to see a doctor after what she says was her fainting spell, and after the discussion about Bobbie's future. Similarly, Alec says to her, after telling her that he has been offered a job in Johannesburg, 'Do you want me to stay? I'll do whatever you say.' Yet to know what her way is, let alone to have it, is what is most difficult for Laura. She is torn between two kinds of desire: passion and duty (which is the desire to do what is right and kind, for 'decency and self-respect'). She is also torn between acceptance of a male value system and a nuanced perception of its inadequacies. All of this is *Brief Encounter*'s feminine angle.

SO ENGLISH
....

Brief Encounter has always been regarded as a quintessentially British film, typical of British cinema and of Britishness itself. This has been its glory but also a stick to beat it with.

It was swiftly heralded, at home and abroad, as the acme of British cinema. There was talk of it representing a 'British school', not only by C.A. Lejeune (who used the phrase) but also by André Bazin (though he retracted his enthusiasm a few years later).[18] It was straightaway a reference point in British writing about film, notably in the work of the *Penguin Film Review* and Roger Manvell, which set the agenda for the serious consideration of cinema in Britain for many years. The script was published (a rare enough accolade) in 1950 as one of *Three British Screenplays* and in 1974 as one of four *Masterworks of the British Cinema*. By the 60s it was also being excoriated for the very same Britishness, by the journal *Movie*, for instance, and in Raymond Durgnat's book *A Mirror for England*. Its place has nonetheless remained secure. There is a still from the film on the cover of Denis Gifford's 1968 'illustrated guide', *British Cinema*, and both on the cover and as a backdrop to the opening pages of a chapter on 'The British Tradition' in Gilbert Adair and Nick Roddick's *A Night at the Pictures: Ten Decades of British Film*, published in 1985 for 'British Film Year'. In such general accounts of British cinema, *Brief Encounter* is taken to be both so well known and so archetypal as to be the obvious emblematic choice. In the Adair and Roddick volume, twenty-one critics (including such specialists in British cinema as Andy Medhurst, Rachael Low, Pam Cook, James Park, Colin McArthur and Charles Barr) were invited to nominate their top ten British films; in the resultant poll of polls, *Brief Encounter* came third.

Beyond this, *Brief Encounter* has also come to be taken as a symbol of Britishness itself. When anglophile Helena Hanff goes to the cinema in Manhattan in the film of *84 Charing Cross Road* (1987), it is a screening of *Brief Encounter* that sets her dreaming longingly of London again (though of course *Brief Encounter* is not set in London, and London is not Britain – the vagueness is the point). It has become part of the contemporary concern with heritage. A still figures on the cover of Nicola Beauman's study of the inter-war British woman's novel, a work concerned (along with its publisher, Virago) to rescue a wealth of British fiction that had been in danger of being consigned to oblivion. Heritage as tourism is equally at home with *Brief Encounter*. More than one disused railway station has been opened up as a *Brief Encounter* tea room, though Carnforth Station in Lancashire, where the film was

BRIEF ENCOUNTER

Wholefood Restaurant

Home cooked vegetarian food —
a healthy and original alternative

in the Award-winning
Victorian station at Great Malvern

Thursday — Friday — Saturday 7pm — 11pm Fully Licensed

Come for a Brief Encounter with us
We are under the clock on Platform 1

Good food — Comfortable surroundings — Friendly atmosphere

BRIEF ENCOUNTER RESTAURANT   Telephone (0684) 893033
Great Malvern Station
Imperial Road off Avenue Road   Malvern   *Booking Advisable*

Flyer for the Brief Encounter restaurant

shot, has slid into decay.

Yet in what sense is *Brief Encounter* so British? I want to argue both that it is not a typical film, more particular and limited than that would suggest, but that it is nonetheless a central one, embodying certain powerful notions of both British cinema and Britishness more generally.

. . . .

In many ways, *Brief Encounter* is not typical of British film-making traditions. On the one hand, one would have to leave out of account so much British cinema – vulgar comedy (George Formby, *Carry Ons*), Gainsborough melodramas, Hammer horror, figures like Hitchcock, Powell and Pressburger, Greenaway, Jarman – if one were to establish a lineage in which *Brief Encounter* would appear typical. And on the other hand, it is not a documentary, so often claimed to be 'Britain's outstanding contribution to the film'.[19]

Yet *Brief Encounter* does exemplify three qualities of a certain strain of British cinema: theatricality, realism and the 'filmic'. I deliberately use the word 'qualities', ambiguously suggesting both characteristic and best, because that is how they figure still in ordinary critical discourse, in broadsheet newspaper reviews, the vocabulary of BAFTA awards or the assumptions students bring to film courses. These qualities constitute for critical common sense both what British cinema does aspire to and, for most, what it also should aspire to. This strain of film-making and these characteristics are part of British cinema; they are by no means the whole story or unchallengeable artistic goals; they do, however, help us to characterise *Brief Encounter*.

Theatricality is the least important of them, as far as this film is concerned, even though it is based on a play (*Still Life*, part of a series of short plays and sketches by Noël Coward called *Tonight at 8.30*, first performed in 1936), much of whose dialogue is retained (though in the play Alec pontificates more and Fred does not appear). The proximity of the British studios to the West End theatre has always been significant for British cinema (compare Hollywood and Broadway with a continent between them), so that certain aspects of this particular theatrical tradition have been influential: the primacy of the verbal, acting understood as having to do (in quite a wide sense) with manners, the assumption of a class continuity between performers and audiences. These aspects do all characterise *Brief Encounter*, because it is a film about people of this class and about manners (how to behave), and, as already discussed, these are particularly important in relation to Celia Johnson's performance. However, they are blended into its realist and filmic qualities so that the film does not look in any other sense theatrical.

One other aspect of theatre may be touched on here, namely the idea of 'well made' drama. Although it uses far from theatrical means to do so, *Brief Encounter* is informed by that ideal of playwriting in which all loose ends are tied up and every detail contributes to the overall thematics of the work. For instance, it doesn't just happen to be set for much of the time in a train station; the setting is central to the tension and meaning of the piece. Roger Manvell noted the symbolic import of the different kinds of train: the 'passing express trains have the rush and power of passion ... [the] local trains jerk and shunt with their faithful service of routine domesticity.'[20] Dilys Powell further noted the way that the timetable rules the lovers' lives: 'They never lose the

The pressure of time: Albert checks his watch, Laura buys a clock

consciousness by which Bradshaw for them appoints that joy has its inexorable end.[21] Time, its pressure, its fleetingness, is endlessly referenced in the film. In the first shots after the credits, Albert checks his fob watch as the express goes by, then glances up at the station clock before going into the buffet; Myrtle says that she cannot be 'wasting time' gossiping and that 'time and tide wait for no man, Mr Godby'; Laura buys an elaborate clock for Fred; Alec says in the boathouse, 'There's no time at all'; Albert checks his watch after taking Laura and Alec's tickets; Alec says, 'We've still got a few minutes', just before Dolly comes crashing in. There are also many interruptions, reminders of time: Dolly's arrival; Albert saying he couldn't meet Myrtle because he had to dash off to a friend's wedding; the bell for the Churley train bringing conversation between Laura, Alec and Dolly to a halt; Fred asking Laura to turn the music down; Stephen coming back early and bursting in on Alec and Laura's tryst. This precise and intricate well-madeness extends, as we shall see, to the titles of the films Alec and Laura go to see and to the clues and answers in Fred's crossword puzzle. The latter might even be emblematic of why some

people dislike the film, a sense of its being honed and created to a point of rigidity like that of a crossword. Yet, as I'll suggest, the life of *Brief Encounter* is in the tension between this well-madeness and the film's emotional currents.

The second quality of the narrow but prestigious strand of British cinema that is relevant to *Brief Encounter* is realism, meaning here the rendering of an observable social world in an unobtrusive manner. This kind of realism privileges the public over the private, the everyday over the exceptional. It is partly a matter of film style but also, in *Brief Encounter* especially, of attitude.

Brief Encounter's realism consists in the first place of its use of location shooting, with important scenes played on station platforms, in parks and on streets, and in interiors including a cinema and (it looks to me) a chemist and a Kardomah. The studio sets are carefully verisimilitudinous. Laura's home is comfortably but not lavishly furnished; prop details (Toby jugs on the mantelpiece, a Cona coffee-maker) seem accurate. Similarly, the station buffet looks clean but lived-in, functional rather than showy. Although a three-sided, rectangular set, its missing fourth wall is one of the short ones, so that the disposition of furniture and the framing do not evoke a long-side-on, proscenium-arched stage set; this is emphasised by the opening camera track, which goes into the room along its length.

Ironically, as Antonia Lant points out, much of the naturalistic detail was in reality faked because of wartime scarcities: dummy packets of chocolate, inedible cakes, plaster fruits and so on. Moreover, on its first showing in postwar austerity Britain, such qualities might provoke nostalgia or giggles for the relative luxury of prewar days. Equally, the patina of detail for us now may be a source of nostalgia or camp – that weird Cona coffee-maker, Laura's endearing soft hats, brandy only ten old pence a nip (about 4p in today's money) and Kardomahs (once so *moderne*).

The apprehension of something as realistic has much to do with what it is not like, that is, other available representations. Much of the praise for *Brief Encounter*'s truth to life was couched in terms of its not being Hollywood ('There is no attempt to hit you over the head with the Hollywood bladder called romance'[22]). The hidden point of reference here and in most discussion of the film – is melodrama. So often *Brief Encounter* is not recognised as melodrama, and I myself hesitated when recommending it for a season of European melodrama at the Swedish Film Institute. Emotion and desire are not carried here in gesturally big, vocally loud performance nor in the kind of tumultuous camerawork and editing of a Griffith or a Minnelli. Nor does it look like contemporaneous British hits such as *The Wicked Lady* and *The Seventh Veil*, which were recognised (and critically disparaged) as melodramas. Yet no film could be more a case of a drama unfolded to music, the literal definition of melodrama – *Brief Encounter* without Rachmaninov is unimaginable. Nor could any film be more about the necessity and impossibility of desire, the clash of the demands of the heart and the limitations of reality, to take contemporary theorists' definition of film melodrama.[23]

In short, no film is more of a melodrama than *Brief Encounter*. Yet the film itself asks not be treated as melodrama but as realism. There is a recurrent mockery of all that melodrama stands for, not just in Hollywood and studios like Gainsborough but in popular culture generally.

Laura's flashback begins as she sits in an armchair opposite husband Fred. The image before her dissolves into that of the buffet; it is as if she is watching the story of her brief encounter on a screen. Yet while this might appear to suggest her memories as 'movies', it ushers in a realism quite at odds with what *Brief Encounter* shows us of actual cinema. Laura is an inveterate filmgoer, yet she disparages most of what she sees, as does the film itself. She is 'sick' of 'those noisy musical things' and *Flames of Passion* is a 'terribly bad picture' which she and Alec leave early. The titles and presentation of the films within the film are mocked. The pair's first choice is between *The Loves of Cardinal Richelieu* (romantic sensationalisation of a political life) and *Love in a Mist*, which sounds like a vapid British comedy. The trailer for *Flames of Passion* is an incoherent compendium of images of desire-as-exotic, with Indian and African natives, villages and dancers, a woman in Pacific print attire and a King Kong ape, all to the accompaniment of extravagant claims ('Stupendous! Epoch-making!') in bold lettering. It is already a comic pastiche, and the film emphasises its absurdity: Alec and Laura exchange ironic looks during the trailer, which is immediately followed by a slide advertising a baby pram, not only prosaic but a reminder of the real price of heterosexual sex. When the couple see the film itself, it turns out to be based on a novel called *Gentle Summer*, suggesting the very opposite of what the movies have made it, by a novelist called Alice Porter Stoughey, who might well be the kind borrowed by Laura from Boots.

Such cinema forms part of a broader popular culture that is also mocked by the film. Dolly talks of the 'passion for doctors' as a kind of female folklore. Laura draws on what Fred calls 'Victorian' imagery in her description of the navy. When she fantasises about being with Alec, she herself mocks as schoolgirlish and silly the standard-issue imagery of Paris, Venice, waltzing, the opera, palm trees, luxury liners and sunsets. She mocks Mrs Leftwich for 'the silliest hat I've ever seen' and Fred chivvies her to hurry up with her make-up ('all this beautifying'). Often the implicit contrast with the real is to hand: a real passion for a doctor as compared to a gossipy one, a modest hat as opposed to a silly one. What all these examples share, of course, is a notion of a specifically feminine popular culture (in which melodrama is always a prize exhibit). Part of *Brief Encounter*'s realism has to do with

Laura's flashback: watching herself on a screen

distinguishing itself from a culture that is both popular and female, a conflation common in accounts of 'mass culture' (often through the image of 'the shopgirl', female purveyor and addict of mass consumption). To return for a moment to the theme of the last chapter, the acceptability to someone like E. Arnot Robertson of *Brief Encounter*'s treatment of women's issues has in large measure to do with its explicit rejection of what cinema most commonly offered as a 'feminine angle'.

The contrasts within the film – passion and prams, silly and sensible headgear – are crucial to its realism in another sense, namely advocating the necessity of accepting lowered horizons, of 'being realistic'. It is central to Laura and Alec's dilemma: 'We must be sensible, please help me to be sensible', 'It's too late now to be as sensible as all that'; and it is reiterated in endless details. The pram gag, for instance, is echoed in two others: Stanley coming in on Myrtle, Albert and the Banburys on the floor, and saying nudgingly, 'Just in Time – or Born in the Vestry'; the two soldiers who twist Myrtle's concern about not 'getting into trouble' to lewd ends ('Just give us a chance, lady!'). I often have to point out these gags to my students,

partly because phrases like 'getting a girl into trouble' no longer have wide currency, but chiefly because anxiety about conception is no longer so hard to extricate from heterosexual sex. These gags are a backdrop of lowering realism to the high passion of romantic desire. Similarly Fred notes, with a barely perceptible *moue* of irony, that 'romance' fits properly between 'delirium' and 'Baluchistan' (madness and foreignness) in his crossword; Alec decides against seeing the *Loves of Cardinal Richelieu* because he was once sick on a boat named after the Cardinal; at the end of her reverie about being with Alec, Laura observes, and the screen shows us, that palm trees inevitably turn into pollarded willows, graceful trees with their branches clipped; and so on.

The realism of *Brief Encounter* consists, then, partly in a certain naturalism of location and set but also in its difference from other representations of desire in film and popular culture, representations it explicitly distances itself from. The realism is both a rejection of certain notions of femininity and also provides the grounding for the articulation of another female tradition, as discussed in the previous chapter. All this would seem to banish the film's melodramatic impulses

'Flames of Passion'

– yet recognition of such impulses is part of the Boots fiction tradition, and the feelings remain in the film, all the more fierce for being so assiduously kept at bay.

If British cinema was enjoined to be realistic, it was also required to be filmic, that is, to use the techniques specific to film as a medium. That great film art must reside in the medium's exploitation of what is peculiar to it was a tenet of much writing about film in the period, most influentially perhaps in Paul Rotha's work;[24] this tenet itself was based on a widespread philosophical conviction that every art should exploit what is essential to it. In film terms, this meant in part building on the medium's capacity for realism (the camera as a recorder of what is put in front of it) but also in emphasising camera position and movement, and editing. Many of the key personnel on *Brief Encounter* – cinematographer Robert Krasker, editor Jack Harris and of course director David Lean himself – were master craftsmen in this tradition.

When applied by critics to *Brief Encounter* being filmic meant praising many set pieces of technique: the extreme close-up on Dolly's mouth as she gossips over Laura's inner misery, the dissolve from the living room to the buffet that ushers in Laura's flashback, the sudden cloud of steam that blows up into Laura's face as she says, 'At that moment the first awful feeling of danger swept over me', Laura looking in the train carriage window at her face as it in turn looks on at her fantasies, the sudden, panicky cut from Alec and Stephen to Laura's feet running through puddles, the tilting camera for Laura's suicide attempt. If, when I first saw *Brief Encounter*, I was captivated by the realist capturing of ordinary middle-class life, it was also these set pieces that I readily pronounced 'brilliant'.

I still find them effective, but the more I have looked at the film the more astounded I am by the highly filmic yet much less obtrusive techniques at work. The first shot of the buffet, for instance, is taken from a quite high (above shoulder level) position, behind the bar and angled towards the entrance. Albert enters (we have already seen him doing so from outside in the previous shot) and the camera moves along part of the length of the bar in the same direction and at the same pace as Alec, who moves away with two cups of tea, and Beryl, who goes to clear a table by the door. It stops when Albert gets to the bar and greets Myrtle with ' 'ullo, 'ullo, 'ullo!' The camera movement draws

Conspicuous technique: close-up of Dolly gossipping over Laura's misery

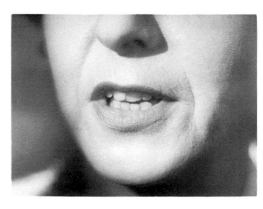

us into the scene, using this uniquely filmic device to create the sense of being 'in' the world of the film. Following the previous shot of Albert, having him walk towards the camera's own movement, and having it stop on him and Myrtle, emphasise these characters, almost as if they are to be the main ones. The camera performs the equivalent of authorial narration, taking the viewer into the scene, directing his/her attention. Yet because the line of the camera's movement follows that of the bar and of Beryl and Alec, and because its pace likewise follows Beryl and Alec, it seems motivated by the simple, non-directive necessity of following on-screen movement.

The shot is not yet finished. The camera moves away from Albert and Myrtle as he begins telling her about the man with a third-class ticket getting out of a first-class compartment and how Mr Saunders 'ticked 'im off proper'; it moves further along the line of the bar, turning slightly, as Beryl comes and puts two cups and saucers on the end; it comes to rest looking over the end of the bar and down on Laura and Alec. Once again line and pace are motivated by movement on screen; once again the film-as-narrator is drawing attention to particular characters. These characters are played by the stars of the film (Celia Johnson, at any rate, already a familiar screen presence); we see their position in relation to the rest of the room and the other characters, that is, slightly separate and marked-off, special. By passing via Albert and Myrtle, the camera both connects and differentiates them from Alec and Laura, a motif throughout the film (see below). The camera has gradually found its way to this space, as if at last coming to what we presume will be the heart of the matter, the private precariously lived on the edge of the public. Yet we don't hear what they say, we are still in the position of frustrated eavesdropper (which will make Laura's eventual confession all the more powerful for us); what we do hear is Albert talking about a miscreant, so that we see the lover from the first through a discourse of guilt, and specifically guilt about cheating.

I find such unobtrusive richness of texture, which is characteristic of the whole film, astonishing. Poring over a sequence like this is what makes film studies exhilaratingly worthwhile. Yet I know that many people find the whole film too deliberate, too crafted. I return to the point about the way in which even Fred's crossword echoes the heart of the plot. If you don't feel the melodramatic pull of the film, then everything fits just a little too neatly and rigidly, the life has been squeezed out of the film by the meticulousness with which it has been put together. But I do feel it.

....

I have discussed *Brief Encounter* as an example of British cinema from the point of view of its textual qualities rather than its place in British picturegoing. Consideration of this will lead us to the question of its Britishness in more general terms.

Although it was not a disaster when it first appeared, *Brief Encounter* was not especially successful. Two other British films released that year, *The Wicked Lady* and *Piccadilly Incident*, both dramas centred on women and involving adultery, were hugely more successful; unusually for home product, the first was the biggest box-office hit of the year and the second was equal runner-up with *The Bells of St. Mary's*. It is hard to be sure just how well *Brief Encounter* did. It does figure in *Kinematograph Weekly*'s list of 'Other Notable Box-office Attractions' for 1946, and when it was re-released in 1948 another trade paper, *To-day's Cinema*, said that there was no need to extol its virtue

The first shot of the buffet

'for showmen are well aware that the film was one of the biggest money-spinners of its year.' David Lean, in an article on the film in the *Penguin Film Review*, claimed that it 'was not a big box-office success' but that all the same it 'did very well ... in what are known as "the better-class halls"'[25] In some ways, the critics did not want it to be a success, since mass approval might suggest the film was coarser than they held it to be. Lejeune was explicit: 'I doubt very much if it will be generally popular. ... Nothing the producers can contrive to do is going to make [it] an understandable film for the practical millions';[26] and Lean offers a familiar sketch of the mass audience unable to appreciate such work, in terms of their immaturity ('The greater proportion of film-goers are under twenty-one mentally or physically') and class and gender, the awful spectre of the shopgirl ('Displease several million Marys and thousands of pounds are down the drain').[27]

If *Brief Encounter*'s appeal to British audiences was, at the very least, considerably less sure than might be expected of a supposedly archetypal British film, then this must throw into doubt the wider claim to its Britishness. To begin with, is it not in any case (as my chapter title has implied all along) rather English than British? In terms of the representation of Scotland and Wales (in other words, leaving aside the question of the actual continuities in middle-class life across Britain), it is difficult to imagine *Brief Encounter* set, with a mere change of accent, in Perth or Llangollen – the absence of religion, of a morality beyond niceness, of hard weather and traditionalism, all suggest English softness and secularism.

This in turn is a specific perception of England. Where the film is set is uncertain. The station exteriors and the countryside were shot in Lancashire, as signs to Lancaster, Leeds, Bradford and Barrow in the station, and the stonework of the bridge in the country, attest. However, the other exteriors (for example, the street, the park, the cinema) were shot in the South, as was all the studio work. It all *feels* very Home Counties, very Guildford or Chingford (or 'Milford'), above all because of the accents, especially those of the working-class characters, who have not a trace of North country about them. Just as England often stands for Britain, so the Home Counties, as here, time and again are taken for England.

Beyond the question of region, the film's class position suggests a narrow idea of Englishness. The main characters' accents, the assumption that ordinariness encompasses having a live-in servant, the class-cultural giveaways of *The Times* crossword, books from Boots and classical music, all suggest that this is not about typical English people at all, but about what was then a minority, the middle class.

In fact many, quite possibly most, popular British (and indeed Hollywood) films were, and still are, about middle- and upper-class people. The major British hits contemporaneous with *Brief Encounter* – *The Wicked Lady*, *Piccadilly Incident* and *The Seventh Veil* – all centre on well-to-do women with servants and the temptations of lovers. Classical music, not just on the soundtrack but in the fictional world of the film itself, was a staple of popular British cinema, whether the established concert repertoire (as in *Forget-Me-Not*, 1936; *Moonlight Sonata*, 1936; *The Common Touch*, 1940; *Millions Like Us*, 1943; *The Magic Bow*, 1945; and *The Seventh Veil*) or specially composed works (*Dangerous Moonlight*, 1941; *Love Story*, 1944; *While I Live*, 1947). Piano concertos in the high romantic mode were particularly common: *Moonlight Sonata*, *The Common Touch* (Tchaikovsky 1), *Dangerous*

'Laura's clothes are not made of expensive and sensual material like Margaret Lockwood's in *The Wicked Lady*'

Moonlight (the 'Warsaw Concerto'), *Love Story* ('Cornish Rhapsody'), *While I Live* ('The Dream of Olwen'), *The Seventh Veil* (various, but including *Brief Encounter*'s Rachmaninov 2). The significance of the concerto, and especially of the woman soloist, for 'women's films' is discussed above.

It is not the mere fact of settings and the music that may make *Brief Encounter* unacceptably middle-class for some audiences (and thus unrepresentatively English). It is rather the precision with which the film invites the audience to identify with a middle-class perspective.

On the one hand, it is studiously unglamorous in its depiction of middle-class life. Laura's clothes are not made of expensive and sensual material like Margaret Lockwood's in *The Wicked Lady*; her home is small, cramped and spare compared to the spaciousness and heavy furnishings that Ann Todd inhabits in *The Seventh Veil*. There is no possibility here of ignoring the class specificity in favour of the gorgeousness of the life style, for its own sake or as a basis for treating the character's feelings and dilemmas as universal ones, stripped of the particularities of class and the problems of immediate material want.

The film's realism makes its middle-classness more alien for many than a glamorous treatment would have done.

On the other hand, *Brief Encounter* also clearly asks the audience to distinguish itself from its working-class characters. This has only partly to do with performance. Joyce Carey's Myrtle is, certainly, a figure of fun, though even her playing is more nuanced than is usually allowed. Beryl is not comic at all, Stanley and the two soldiers who cheek Myrtle make jokes rather than being funny characters, and Stanley Holloway, a well established music-hall star, surely invites us to laugh with rather than at Albert. However, these characters are sources of amusement for Laura and so are meant to be for us.

Myrtle, Albert and the rest are set up as a show for Laura. The dissolve that starts her flashback puts Myrtle and Albert centre-screen; Laura in her armchair both looks directly at them and refers to Myrtle as a familiar source of amusement ('The woman at the counter was going on as usual, the one with the refined voice'). Laura at home fades from view; we are now in the flashback. When Alec passes her table she looks down and away from him momentarily but then looks up again at Albert and Myrtle, smiling to herself, as they go into what amounts to a sketch. In a later scene, when Alec has brought buns to the table, Laura gestures to him to be quiet and enjoy the show: Myrtle telling Beryl about leaving her husband. The film cuts to this, and when she has finished, on the punch-line 'Dead as a doornail inside three years', cuts back to Alec and Laura smiling ironically to each other before turning their attention away. When Laura is next by herself in the buffet, she sits facing the stove, so that when Myrtle bends over to shovel coal into it and Albert comes in and slaps her bottom they are directly in Laura's line of vision; again, the film cuts back to Laura, smiling in amusement at this by-play. More badinage follows, culminating in the Banburys all over the floor, and the film again cuts back to Laura looking on ironically, insisting on them as a spectacle for her amusement.

The role of the lower, especially the servant, classes as a foil to the serious affairs of their betters is a standard one in Western theatrical tradition. Here their affairs are not only a comic version of Alec and Laura's, but also, as I have mentioned, a suggestion of an alternative to it, more free and easy, careless, possibly enviable.

This is particularly suggestive in the character of Beryl, Myrtle's underling, in the scene when Laura returns from wandering the streets after fleeing Stephen's flat. Beryl is on her own with the buffet to close and her boyfriend Stanley to see (as Laura comes in, he tells Beryl he'll wait for her in the yard). Laura puts a brake on Beryl's job and love life, coming in late, demanding not just brandy but paper and envelope, which the buffet does not normally provide, and then, when Alec arrives, hanging on beyond closing time. In a production of *Still Life* I saw at the Birmingham Rep in 1970, a friend of mine, Theresa Watson, played the part of Beryl and managed to suggest that here was a woman equally as worthy of consideration as Laura, whose desire to be with Stanley was just as urgent as Laura's to be (and not to be) with Alec. This was quiet playing against the grain of the play, and I don't think that either play or film – or Laura – intends us to have this perception, but even in the film Beryl is not a comic character, nor a sideshow. In the play, Albert refers to Alec and Laura slightly disparagingly as 'Romeo and Juliet'; the way, in the film, Margaret Barton as Beryl leans back on a table and plays with the keys as she watches Laura and Alec leave, could suggest that she has the same amused sense of superiority to them. At one point immediately after, when Alec and Laura are walking along the platform and he is telling her about Johannesburg, they fall silent and Beryl and Stanley run giggling loudly down the underpass behind them, an expression of free high spirits that contrasts with Alec and Laura's repressed agonies. This is not something Alec and Laura contemplate for amusement but something going on elsewhere, registered but not set up by Laura in her memory. By this stage in the film, for all the patronisation of the working-class characters, there is surely also a sense of envy – but one which still assumes that the viewer too will not be a Beryl.

Brief Encounter insistently distances itself and Laura from its working-class characters. This does not mean that it has to be taken this way. The excess of Beryl and Stanley's high spirits is exhilarating. Stanley Holloway was a beloved performer, whose warm humour may have been more sympathetic to many than Alec's snotty wittiness about female musicians and Donald Duck. A friend has told me how many of her working-class students see in Myrtle an economically independent woman able, unlike Laura, to leave her husband, still be respectable and handle Albert's advances on her own terms. Yet such responses go against the grain of the film, which if anything draws attention to the treatment of the lower class as a function of upper-class sensibility, and within a claim to realism. It is this that has made audiences so often uncomfortable with both Albert and Myrtle *and* Laura.

This quintessentially British film was, then, not hugely successful with British audiences and is indelibly marked as middle-class, Home Counties English. Yet this voice – after all, that of the BBC, of our déclassé monarchy, of Churchill during the Second World War – has often presented itself as the voice of the nation, and been accepted as

such by many who do not speak in this voice. A nation's characteristic culture may on inspection usually be a narrow and class-specific one, but it is nonetheless what passes for the national culture.

When Laura sits in despair at the war memorial, one could take it, as Jackie Stacey suggested to me, as an image of the nation. There is something oddly abstract and emblematic about the overhead shots here, partly because there is no other camera position as high as this in the film, partly because the studio set lacks the patina of realism caught or constructed so assiduously elsewhere in the film. The war memorial is not only patriarchal, as discussed above, but also national, and this is especially suggestive in a film released at the end of the war. As Jackie Stacey puts it, it is as if Laura holds the fate of the nation in her hands. Her return to Fred will signal a return to normality, the normality the war was fought to protect, a normality which includes the return of women to the home after the unusual experience (the romance) of working away from it.

A feature of this nation is that it is a white one. *Brief Encounter* is not making a point about this – white films seldom know that they are about whiteness – yet its Englishness is a specifically white construction. I'd like to relate here a curious experience of using the film in the context of a course concerned with issues of ethnic representation. I wanted to show a film that would provide a basis for trying to talk about images of white people, but wanted to avoid one that was explicitly about race and thereby allowed a white audience to see white characters' whiteness (as we usually cannot) by means of a contrast with a non-white identity. I wanted to see if we could acknowledge whiteness when there were only white people on screen. I chose *Brief Encounter* because any film with only white people in it would do and it might as well be one of my favourites.

The most striking thing that emerged from this viewing and the subsequent discussion, however, was the significance of reference to non-white cultures. Dolly talks of the dangers of Africa (a woman who had 'the most dreadful time . . . all her hair came out and she said the social life was quite, quite horrid'); romance, in Fred's crossword, 'fits' with delirium and Baluchistan (then part of India); *Flames of Passion* is an amalgam of African, Asian and Pacific imagery; Laura's 'schoolgirl' fantasies drift from Europe to palm trees and tropical moonlight; and

Alec is leaving to take up a job in Johannesburg. Always the non-white represents excitement, but also its dangers and foolishness. Only Johannesburg in South Africa – then perceived as a securely white territory – represents renunciation and practicality, but also, as colonised land, an available space for the resolution of white people's dilemmas. It seemed from our discussion of the film as if white identities are ineluctably dependent on non-white for their existence, so that even a film with only white characters in it has to have recourse to non-white reference to convey the boundaries of whiteness. However, we were predominantly a group of white people – perhaps still all we could 'see' of whiteness were those boundaries?

It is possible, yet problematic, to go further than this. If one tries to put some characteristics to the representation of whiteness, to give whiteness some actual stereotypical attributes rather than treating it as merely non-black or non-coloured, one is likely to come up with terms like controlled, rational, orderly, repressed, cerebral, stiff, uptight and so on. There are two problems with such a description, recognisable though it is. One is that, even at the level of representation, it is far from covering all images of white people. After all, Albert, Myrtle and Beryl are just as white as Laura, Alec and Fred, and yet the former exactly lack the control and so on of the latter. Secondly, but related to the first problem, these attributes are also the ones that get applied to the upper class or to men, so that the specificity of the characteristics of whiteness is merged with that of other dominant groups. *Brief Encounter*'s construction of Englishness is a white one and it is especially important to say so in contemporary multi-ethnic Britain, yet it is still hard to give that whiteness much content.

. . . .

Brief Encounter's Englishness is something very specific and limited, but if I try to put my finger on why *Brief Encounter* affects me so, it is this Englishness that seems to get it best. The appeal for me has something to do with nostalgia for a way of life that my family aspired to yet never quite inhabited. It has, though, mainly to do with the way the film handles emotions, the heartbreakingly touching awkwardness of its characters, what Laura describes as the English being so 'shy and difficult'. In fact this quality may be found in such nationally diverse films as *Tokyo Story*, *The Man Who Shot Liberty Valance* and *Babette's Feast*, but then perhaps it is very 'English' of me to love those films too.

It is common to characterise this way with emotions as inhibited or even emotionless. The English are cold fish with stiff upper lips. Yet this is to mistake restraint for repression and lack of expression for lack of feeling. To see *Brief Encounter* as only cups of tea, banal conversation and guilt is not really to see or hear it at all. When Laura praises Alec for behaving 'so beautifully' when Dolly joins them in their last moments together, praises him because 'no one could have guessed what he was feeling', this does not give us a warrant to fail to see (to 'guess') why Alec and Laura act with restraint or how much and deeply they feel.

On the one hand, their – and especially Laura's – holding back from going with their longing for one another is not just con-ventionality or inhibition, but also a sense of affection and loyalty to others, a desire not to hurt anyone. Such niceness is for women indeed inextricable from the internalised address of patriarchy that I discussed above – Laura's unheard confession to Fred begins by saying that she can't tell him because he would be hurt 'and oh, my dear, I don't want you to be hurt'. The sense of English restraint being to do with gentleness and consideration for others may also be felt to sit ill with the actual record of British imperialism. It is an illusory ideal – but not an unattractive or contemptible one.

Such restraint is not the absence of feeling. Indeed, there can be no concept of restraint without an acknowledgment of feeling – restraint must keep something emotional in check. In *Brief Encounter* the gestures the characters make, what they say and how they say it, are seldom overtly and directly expressive (though Alec's declaration of love and Laura's 'I can't go on' speech are in fact very direct), but there is a huge pressure of emotion in a myriad flat or tiny details: in her saying to Alec, after she has so obviously fallen for him as he talks of his specialism, 'It's been so very nice – I've enjoyed my afternoon enormously'; in Alec's pressing Laura's shoulder to say goodbye for the last time; behind Laura's eyes in every close-up of her.

This sense of the pressure of emotion is partly there because one knows to read it there, because that is how emotions are in so much British (white, middle-class, English) culture. It is also because so much in the construction of the film, especially the use of music, Laura's narration and many filmic devices, puts it there. There is a tension here. The film's realism and its careful, for some too careful, filmic craft are themselves restrained, down to earth, in a sense well-mannered. Yet what they deal with is melodrama: characters who feel themselves on an emotional precipice, surging romantic music, encroaching chiaroscuro lighting, stylistically obvious moments of climax (clouds of steam, sudden cuts, tilting camera). In part the organisation contains the melodrama, keeps it at bay with irony and well-mannered distance, but only in part. It also, in the very act of distancing, invokes the power of what has to be kept at bay, the scale of the emotions in play. At the same time, the politeness (of the characters and the style), the irony, the 'being realistic', always keep regret, ruefulness and melancholy to the fore. This seems to me a particular way of handling emotion characteristic of a particular, once, perhaps still, hegemonic, definition of Englishness.

Part of the pleasure of *Brief Encounter* is simply the recognition of the way that restraint, not wanting to hurt, wanting to be nice, desiring comfort, stymie emotional abandon. The very familiarity of this for some people is a pleasure because it confirms part of how we experience our affective lives. There is an extra pull for me too in what I think of as a nostalgia for ordinariness: unlike some gay men, I have never wanted to be marginal and outcast, but have no option. In this perspective the very dowdiness of *Brief Encounter* evokes the cosy lure of normality.

Yet if *Brief Encounter* recognises the difficulty of going with one's feelings for a certain strain of Englishness, it also recognises the strain, fully registers the surging of emotion. It is because of both the social pressures toward and the genuine appeal of comfy conformity, both so meticulously realised, that the desire to love against the grain comes across so powerfully. Moreover, *Brief Encounter*'s recourse to music and to filmic devices also suggests, in this quite extraordinarily verbal film, the limitations of everyday speech to express emotion. Far from lacking emotion, the film is throbbing with it but also registering that emotion cannot be pinned down, summed up, that emotion is overwhelming. That is why *Brief Encounter* is not only a 'lovely', but also a vibrantly 'good' film.

'The pressure of emotion'

NOTES

·······················

1 Andy Medhurst, 'That Special Thrill: *Brief Encounter*, homosexuality and authorship', *Screen*, vol. 32 no. 2, Summer 1991, p. 204.
2 Sue Aspinall, 'Women, Realism and Reality, 1943–53', in James Curran and Vincent Porter (eds.), *British Cinema History* (London: Weidenfeld and Nicolson, 1983), p. 274.
3 Antonia Lant, *Blackout: Reinventing women for wartime British cinema* (Princeton: Princeton University Press, 1991), p. 192.
4 Catherine de la Roche, 'That "Feminine Angle"', *Penguin Film Review* 8, 1949, pp. 25–34.
5 E. Arnot Robertson, 'Woman and the Film', *Penguin Film Review* 3, 1947, p. 32.
6 Catherine de la Roche, 'The Mask of Realism', *Penguin Film Review* 7, 1948, pp. 35–43.
7 Marcia Landy, *British Genres: Cinema and Society, 1930–1960* (Princeton: Princeton University Press, 1991), p. 228.
8 Kate Fleming, *Celia Johnson: A biography* (London: Weidenfeld and Nicolson, 1991), p. 142.
9 Reprinted in Anthony Lejeune (ed.), *The C.A. Lejeune Reader* (Manchester: Carcanet, 1991), p. 233.
10 Fleming, *Celia Johnson*, pp. 99, 101, 140, 142.
11 Quoted ibid., p. 148.
12 Ibid., p. 25.
13 See Nicola Beauman, *A Very Great Profession: The woman's novel 1914–1939* (London: Virago, 1983), pp. 10, 174.
14 Ibid., p. 4.
15 Ibid., p. 201.
16 Rosamund Lehmann, *A Note in Music* (London: Virago, 1982), pp. 62–3. (First published, London: Chatto and Windus, 1930.)

17 Alison Light, *Forever England: Femininity, literature and conservatism between the wars* (London: Routledge, 1991), pp. 210, 163.
18 André Bazin, *Qu'est-ce que le cinéma?* IV (Paris: Les Éditions du Cerf, 1962), p. 47. (This includes both his original view and his retraction of it.)
19 The phrase is from The Arts Enquiry, *The Factual Film* (London: PEP/Oxford University Press, 1947) and is discussed in Andrew Higson, ' "Britain's Outstanding Contribution to the Film": The documentary-realist tradition' in Charles Barr (ed.), *All Our Yesterdays: 90 Years of British Cinema* (London: British Film Institute, 1986), pp. 72–97.
20 Roger Manvell, *The Film and the Public* (Harmondsworth: Penguin, 1955), p. 157.
21 Dilys Powell in George Perry (ed.), *The Dilys Powell Reader* (London: Pavilion, 1989), p. 54. (Review originally published in 1945.)
22 Ion Hammond, *This Year of Film* (London: Dewynter, 1945), p. 32.
23 See especially Christine Gledhill's introduction to her *Home is Where the Heart is: Studies in melodrama and the woman's film* (London: British Film Institute, 1987), but also Sam Rhodie's discussion of *Rocco and his Brothers* in relation to melodrama and realism in his book in this series (London: British Film Institute, 1993).
24 See Tom Ryall, *Alfred Hitchcock and the British Cinema* (London: Croom Helm, 1986), pp. 13–23.
25 David Lean, '*Brief Encounter*', *Penguin Film Review* 4, 1946, pp. 27, 31.
26 C.A. Lejeune, *Chestnuts in her Lap* (London: Phoenix, 1947), p. 162.
27 Lean, '*Brief Encounter*', pp. 27, 29.

CREDITS

....

Brief Encounter

GB
1945
Production company
Nöel Coward-Cineguild
GB trade show
13 November 1945
GB release
11 February 1946
Distributor
Eagle-Lion
US release
24 August 1946
Distributor
Universal
Producer
Noël Coward
In charge of production
Anthony Havelock-Allan,
Ronald Neame
Production manager
Ernest J. Holding
Director
David Lean
Assistant director
George Pollock
Second assistant director
Victor Wark
Third assistant director
Chick Simpson
Screenplay
Noël Coward, David Lean,
Anthony Havelock-Allan
from 'Still Life' in *Tonight at
8.30* by Noël Coward

Continuity
Margaret Sibley
Photography (b & w)
Robert Krasker
Camera operator
Bunny Franke
Additional photography
Ronald Neame
Focus puller
Arthur Ibbetson
Clapper loaders
E. Owen, A. Bryce
Back projection operator
Charles Staffel
Music
Rachmaninov Piano
Concerto No. 2 played by
Eileen Joyce, with the
National Symphony
Orchestra, conducted by
Muir Mathieson
Editor
Jack Harris
Associate editor
Marjorie Saunders
Assistant editor
Winston Ryder
Second assistant editor
J. Cooke
Art director
L.P. Williams
**Artistic supervisor for
Noël Coward**
G.E. Calthorp
Assistant art director
Elven Webb
Draughtsmen
William Lenner, Harry
Westbrook, R. Field-Smith
Scenic decorator
George Demaine

Sound editor
Harry Miller
Sound recordists
Stanley Lambourne,
Desmond Dew
Sound camera operator
Harry Raynham
Boom operator
E. Clennell
Assistant boom operator
M. Stolowitz
Dubbing
Alan Whatley
Location manager
T. Tomson
86 minutes
7,713 feet
Available on VHS in the UK
on the Rank Classics label.

Celia Johnson
Laura Jesson
Trevor Howard
Dr Alec Harvey
Stanley Holloway
Albert Godby
Joyce Carey
Myrtle Bagot
Cyril Raymond
Fred Jesson
Everley Gregg
Dolly Messiter
Marjorie Mars
Mary Norton
Margaret Barton
Beryl Waters
Dennis Harkin
Stanley
Valentine Dyall
Stephen Lynn
Nuna Davey
Mrs Rolandson
Irene Handl
Organist
Edward Hodge
Bill
Sydney Bromley
Johnnie

Wilfred Babbage
Policeman
Avis Scott
Waitress
Henrietta Vintcent
Margaret Jesson
Richard Thomas
Bobbie Jesson
George V. Sheldon
Clergyman
Wally Bosco
Doctor
Jack May
Boatman

The print of *Brief Encounter*
screened at the Museum of
the Moving Image derives
from material deposited
with the National Film and
Television Archive by the
Rank Organisation.

BIBLIOGRAPHY

1. Script
The script has been published with others in Roger Manvell (ed.), *Three British Screenplays* (London: Methuen, 1950) and John Russell Taylor (ed.), *Masterworks of the British Cinema* (London: Lorrimer, 1974), and separately (London: Lorrimer, 1974, 1984). It differs in many small details from the dialogue and action in the film itself and all quotes in my text are from the film, not the published script.

2. Studies
Aspinall, Sue. 'Women, Realism and Reality in British Films, 1943–53' in James Curran and Vincent Porter (eds.), *British Cinema History* (London: Weidenfeld and Nicolson, 1983).

Beauman, Nicola. *A Very Great Profession: The woman's novel 1914–1939* (London: Virago, 1983).

De la Roche, Catherine. 'The Mask of Realism', *Penguin Film Review* 7, 1948, pp. 35–43.

Fleishman, Avrom. *Narrated Films* (Baltimore: Johns Hopkins University Press, 1992).

Landy, Marcia. *British Genres: Cinema and Society, 1930–1960* (Princeton: Princeton University Press, 1991).

Lant, Antonia. *Blackout: Reinventing women for wartime British cinema* (Princeton: Princeton University Press, 1991).

Lean, David. '*Brief Encounter*', *Penguin Film Review* 4, 1946, pp. 27–35.

Light, Alison. *Forever England: Femininity, literature and conservatism between the wars* (London: Routledge, 1991).

Medhurst, Andy. 'That Special Thrill: *Brief Encounter*, homosexuality and authorship', *Screen*, vol. 32 no. 2, Summer 1991, pp. 197–208.